Hi! Welcome to the Irwin Aerobic Party

It's fun to exercise and even more fun to exercise with your friends. The whole gang is here to help you get fit as a fiddle.

All you need to get started is comfortable roomy clothes, a well ventilated room with space enough to move freely and with access to a record or tape player.

Now it's time to get down to it. Feel the music — let yourself go and keep moving. You'll soon discover total fitness is fun.

Coloring Book Too!

IRWIN: Hi, everyone — this is your friend Irwin the Dynamic Duck — presenting your new friend — me — Irwin the Dynamic Aerobic Dancing Duck! Welcome to Irwin's Aerobic Dancing Party.

DONALD THE DISCO FROG: I don't get it, Irwin — what's with this aerobic dancing bit?

IRWIN: Donald! Donald the Disco Frog, glad you came to the party, ole buddy!

DONALD: I'm kinda into dancing myself, ya know — disco 'n all?

IRWIN: You're the greatest!

DONALD: But aerobic dancing? — Never heard of it!

SQUEAK: That's because you never visited MY planet, Mairzy Doats — it's big up there! — Eek!

IRWIN: Squeak!

SQUAWK: Yeah — real big! — Awk!

IRWIN: And Squawk! Squeak and Squawk, my rock-star buddies from outer space!

SQUAWK: When we heard you earth persons had finally caught up with what we've been doing on **Mairzy Doats** for years, we thought we'd drop in and maybe give you a hand —

IRWIN: Hey, I'm gonna take you fellas up on that. But first let's introduce Donald to aerobic dancing with this great old aerobic dancing favorite — Chicken Fat.

Chicken Fat

DONALD: So this is aerobic dancing! Ve-ry interesting.
IRWIN: Hey, great! That was a really great warm-up!
DONALD: Yeah — it was really cookin'!
CLEM THE COOKIE GOBBLER: Cookie? Cookie? Me want cookie?
IRWIN: Clem! Clem the Cookie Gobbler, here at my aerobic dancing party!
CLEM: Any kind cookie, big cookie, small cookie, aerobic dancing cookie, just gimme cookie!
IRWIN: Okay, Clem — just join in on the dancing and you'll get your cookie —
CLEM: MM-M-MM, yeah! Me dance for cookie!
IRWIN: Great, Clem — you can strut your stuff to a record that's made to order for every red-blooded aerobic dancer — Physical! Take it SQUEAK!
SQUEAK: Yeah — eek!
IRWIN: You too, Squawk!
SQUAWK: Of course — let's go! Awk!
DONALD: Say, Irwin, mind if I join in on this routine?
IRWIN: Hey, Donald — sure! Hop in any time you're ready —
DONALD: Ver-ry funny!

TOUCH DOWN
Stand straight, feet together. Touch your toes — 10 times.

PUSH UPS
Lie face down on the floor. Have arms at your side, palms down and elbows bent up keeping body straight push yourself up with your arms and lower yourself down.

MODIFIED PUSH UPS
Lie face down on the floor. Have arms at your side, palms down and elbows bent up. Pushing yourself up with your arms just raise your upper body to your knees and lower yourself down.

Physical

SQUAWK: Okay! Here we go—we're going to do body bounces! Stand with your feet apart, hands on your hips, and bend forward. Now without moving your feet, bounce your body up and down from the waist. Okay?—Now—bounce FRONT—1-2-3-4-5-6-7-8—RIGHT—1-2-3-4-5-6-7-8—BACK—1-2-3-4-5-6-7-8—LEFT—1-2-3-4-5-6-7-8—

SQUEAK: This one's dedicated to you, Irwin, the Irwin stretch!

IRWIN: I'm flattered!

SQUEAK: Stand up tall, arms straight overhead, feet together, keep knees straight, and touch your toes, knees, shoulders and up, toes, knees, shoulders and up, toes, knees, shoulders and up, toes, knees, shoulders and up.

DONALD: This sure is fun, Irwin!

IRWIN: I knew you'd like it, Donald.

SQUAWK: Okay—now—lunges! To your RIGHT—1-2-3-4-5-6-7-8—feet together, lunge LEFT—1-2-3-4-5-6-7-8—feet together, RIGHT FRONT—1-2-3-4-5-6-7-8—feet together, LEFT front—1-2-3-4-5-6-7-8—good!

SQUEAK: And now back to the Irwin stretch—touch toes, knees, shoulders and up, toes, knees, shoulders and up—oh yeah! You're really into it now! Keep it going!

DONALD: Irwin?

IRWIN: Yeah Donald—

DONALD: Think it's okay if I do the calling on jumping jacks and frog jumps? My kinda thing, ya know—

IRWIN: Of course, Donald—go, man go!

DONALD: Okay! Let's get jumpin' with jumping jacks! 1-2-3-4-5-6-7-8—and now FROG JUMPS—touch the FLOOR—JUMP UP—touch the FLOOR—JUMP UP—two more times—yeah—and let's wind up with my favorite, the Irwin stretch! Touch your toes, knees, shoulders and up—toes, knees, shoulders and up—hey, hey, hey! Oh yeah—keep it movin'—toes, knees, shoulders and up—good, good, good!

BODY BOUNCES
Stand with your feet apart. Hands on hips, and bend forward without moving your feet bounce your body up and down from the waist. First bounce front—8 times. Bounce back—8 times. Bounce left—8 times. Bounce right—8 times.

IRWIN STRETCH
Stand straight feet together, arms straight overhead. Bend over keeping knees straight touch toes, then knees, then shoulders and stretch arms overhead—10 times.

LUNGES
Stand straight, feet together. With your right foot step forward (only one step now) and bounce—8 times. Feet together. With your left foot step forward (only one step now like before) and bounce—8 times.

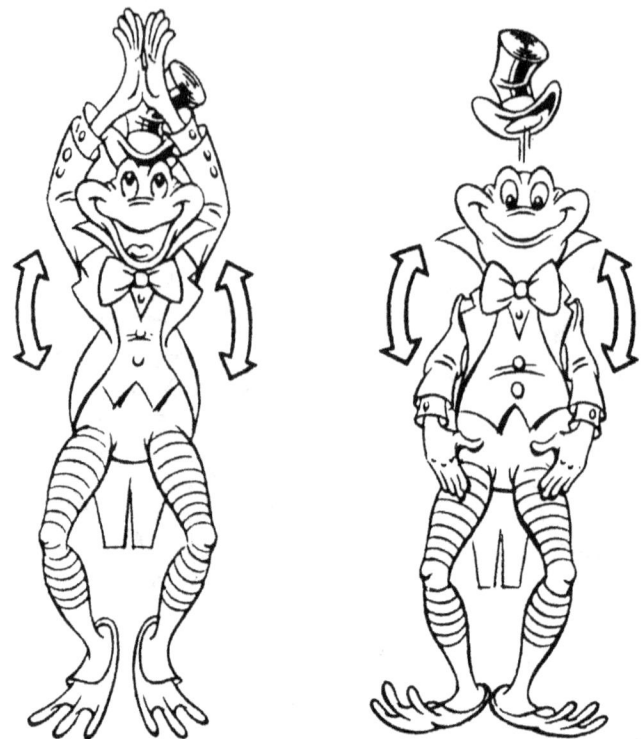

JUMPING JACKS
Stand straight, feet together, arms at sides. When you jump up raise your arms overhead and clap hands together, at the same time spread legs apart sideways. Jump up again, bring arms down to sides and at the same time bring legs together—8 times.

FROG JUMPS
Squat down to the floor with hands touching the floor. Jump up—2 times.

Cotton Eyed Joe

IRWIN: That was great, Donald — and Clem, you were sensational!
CLEM: I get cookie now?
IRWIN: You betcha — here you are!
CLEM: MM-MM cookie! Good, good, good, MM-MM —
IRWIN: Well, whaadaya know! Hey, everybody, look who's here — Barney the Book Bear! Hi ya, Barney, ole buddy!
BARNEY: Hi, Irwin, hi everybody!
IRWIN: Glad you could tear yourself away from all those books long enough to join us, Barney —
BARNEY: Yeah, and look who I brought with me!

IRWIN: Well, I don't believe it — Dr. Swan! Here at an aerobic dancing party!
DR. SWAN: Well, why not, Irwin? Anybody with the name Swan ought to be a pretty good **hand** at dancing! Us Swans kinda have a patent on being graceful, don't cha know!
IRWIN: Okay, touche! And now, in honor of the good doctor and our good buddy, Barney the **Book** Bear, we're going country, with that good old country hoe-down swinger, Cotton Eyed Joe!
DR. SWAN: ER-A-A-HEM! I say, Irwin ole buddy I think I've got the perfect person to do the calling on this one —
IRWIN: Oh year, Dr. Swan? Who?

COUNTRY JIG
Stand straight, feet together. Point with right heel — then point with right toe. Skip to the right 4 times. Point with left heel — then point with left toe. Skip to the left 4 times. Now repeat with the left foot — then the right foot. Skip to your right 4 times clap, clap. Skip to your left 4 times, clap, clap.

SWAN: Me! Who else?
IRWIN: Who else indeed! Go, Man!
DR. SWAN: Here we go with country jig! Heel toe, heel toe, skip 1-2-3-4. Heel toe, heel toe, skip 1-2-3-4. Heel toe, heel toe, skip 1-2-3-4. Thats it — That's good, skip 1-2-3-4.

Skip to your right 1-2-3-4-5-6-clap, clap. Skip to your left 1-2-3-4-5-6-clap, clap.

Jump crosses! Jump cross, jump cross, jump cross, jump cross. Good — that's it! Jump cross, jump cross, jump cross — very nice!

Country jig! Heel toe, heel toe, skip 1-2-3-4. Heel toe, heel toe, skip 1-2-3-4. Heel toe, heel toe, skip 1-2-3-4. Good-good skip 1-2-3-4.

Skip to your right 1-2-3-4-5-6-clap, clap. Skip to your left 1-2-3-4-5-6-clap, clap.

Jump crosses! Jump cross, jump cross, jump cross, jump cross, jump cross — hey, good — very good! Jump cross, jump cross, very nice!

Country jig! Heel toe, heel toe, skip 1-2-3-4. Heel toe, heel toe, skip 1-2-3-4. Heel toe, heel toe, skip 1-2-3-4.

Skip to your right, 1-2-3-4-5-6-clap, clap. Skip to your left, 1-2-3-4-5-6-clap, clap.

Jump crosses! Jump cross, jump cross, jump cross, jump cross. Yeah, good — very good.

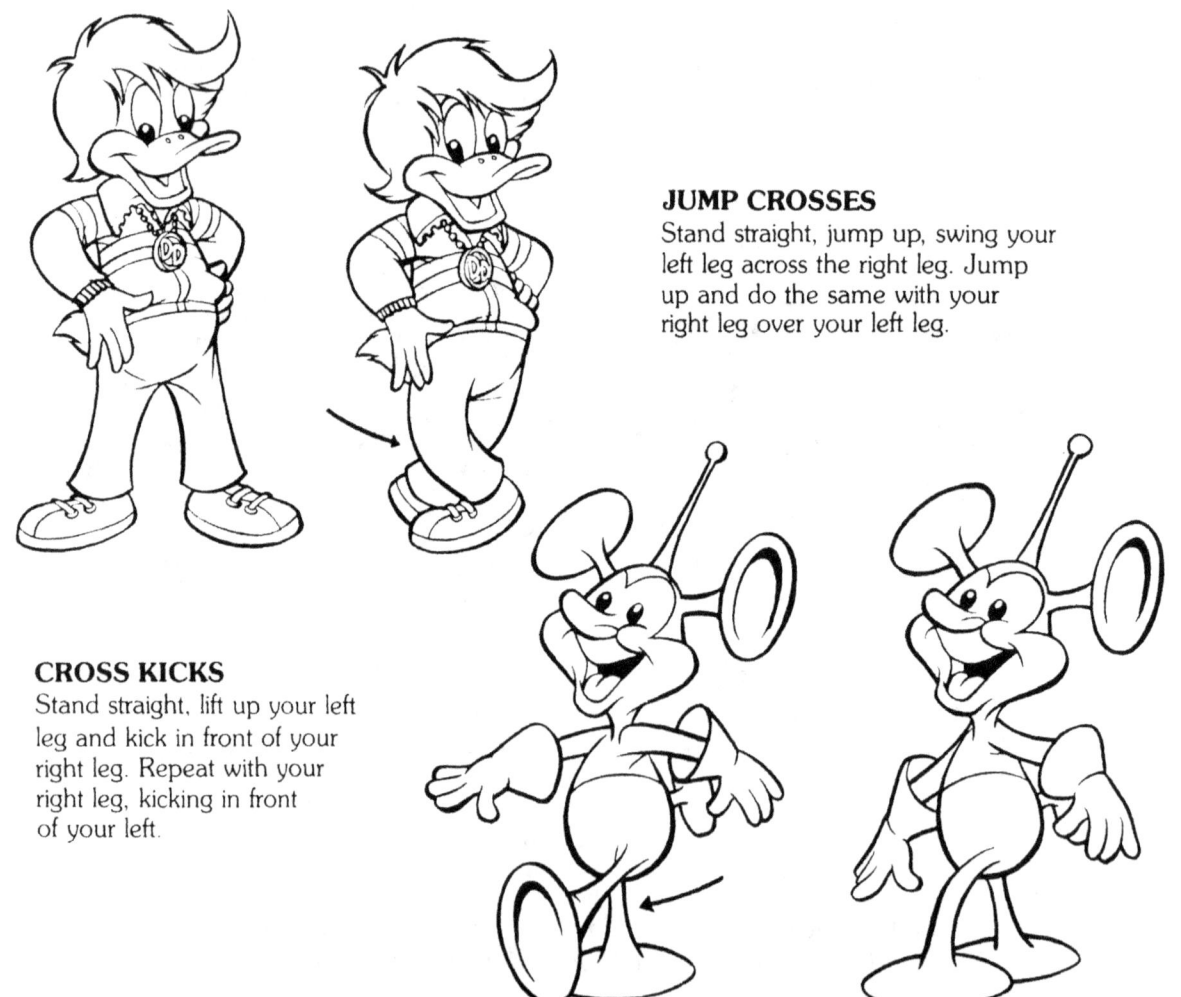

JUMP CROSSES
Stand straight, jump up, swing your left leg across the right leg. Jump up and do the same with your right leg over your left leg.

CROSS KICKS
Stand straight, lift up your left leg and kick in front of your right leg. Repeat with your right leg, kicking in front of your left.

Double Dutch Bus

IRWIN: Dr. Swan, you are somethin' else! Like the greatest, man! Excuse me, folks — someone at the door — hey PETER!
PETER: Hi, Irwin!
IRWIN: And PAN!
PAN: Hi, Irwin, sorry we're late — the bus was late.
IRWIN: That's okay — hey everybody — I want you to meet two very special friends of mine, Peter and Pan!
ALL: Hi, hi there, hello.
SQUEAK: Nice to meet you, Peter person and Pan person!
SQUAWK: Yeah, we've met duck persons and frog persons and swan persons and like that — but you're the first real PEOPLE persons we've ever met!
PAN: As the first people persons YOU'VE ever met, we're delighted to be talking to the first SPACE persons WE'VE ever met!
IRWIN: ALL right! Let's get it moving again! And here's one bus that's always right on time — come on, everybody, climb aboard the DOUBLE DUTCH BUS.

IRWIN: Ohh — yeah! This is a bee-YOOty! Take it, Squeak and Squawk!
SQUAWK: Right! When I give the word, we're gonna jog, like it's a beautiful day and we're out in the morning sun! O — kay! Let's jog! — Yeah — That's it — Like joggin' in the park —

AND NOW — STEP KICKS!

SQUEAK: Wow — That's good — Almost as good as they do it back home on Mairzy Doats — eek!
SQUAWK: Yeah — earth persons learn pretty quick awk! — And now we're gonna skip, like kids coming home after school — ready? SKIP! — good — good — just keep it going! — And now — FROG JUMPS! Down — up — down — up — down — up — down — up — and now — jog! And STEP KICK — and skip — and FROG JUMPS — down — up — down — up — down — up — down — up — and now — jumping jacks — 1-2-3-4-5-6-7-8 — and — jog!

JOGGING
Stand straight run lightly in place.

STEP SWINGS
Stand straight, lift up your left leg and kick in front of your right leg. Repeat with your right leg kicking in front of your left.

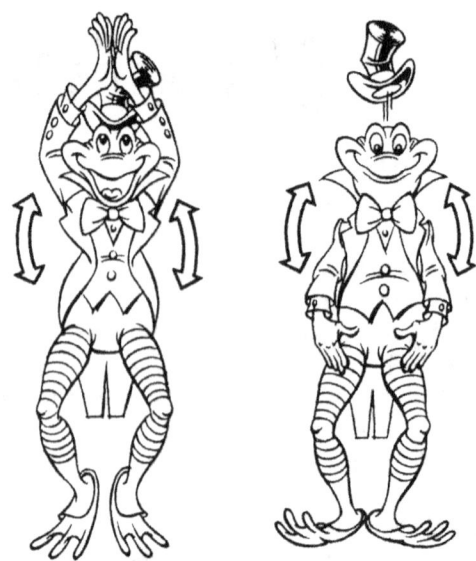

CROSS KICKS
Stand straight, lift up your left leg and kick in front of your right leg. Repeat with your right leg kicking in front of your left.

JUMPING JACKS
Stand straight, feet together, arms at sides. When you jump up raise your arms overhead and clap hands together, at the same time spread legs apart sideways. Jump up again, bring arms down to sides and at the same time bring legs together — 8 times.

FROG JUMPS
Squat down to the floor with hands touching the floor. Jump up — 2 times.

PacMan Fever

IRWIN: Oh, yeah! NOW you've got it — you SURE got it!
DONALD: Got what, Irwin?
IRWIN: The fever, Donald, the fever!
DONALD: The fever? The FEVER??? Lemme outa here!
IRWIN: Nothing to be afraid of, Donald — this is one fever everybody loves to get — it's catchy, it's contagious, it's everywhere — it's Pac Man Fever!
DONALD: Phew! Had me kinda worried there for a minute!
SQUAWK: Well, here's the best thing you can do if you're ever worried — everybody — jog!
SQUAWK: Okay — now let's do those cross-kicks! — Hey, hey, hey, — yeah! — And now, frog jumps! Down — up — down — up — down — up — and jog!
DONALD: Whoo-wee! This is the life!
PETER: Sure is! Hey Squawk, can I get in on this?
SQUAWK: Any time, Peter — be my guest — awk!
PETER: Okay! Now cross-kicks! — Fantastic — what a group! And frog jumps! Down — up — down — up — down — up — down — up — Step swings! Step right, left, right, left, right, left, right, left — jog — that's terrific! And cross kicks!
SQUAWK: Hey, Peter, you're doing real good!
PETER: Thank you! And now, frog jumps — down — up — down — up — that's great — yeah! — and — jumping jacks! 1-2-3-4-5-6-7-8 and jog! Wow! Beautiful!
IRWIN: Yeah! That was tremendous! Tell ya what — let's take a little break, but get right back, 'cause there's lots more comin'!

JOGGING
Stand straight run lightly in place.

CROSS KICKS
Stand straight, lift up your left leg and kick in front of your right leg. Repeat with your right leg kicking in front of your left.

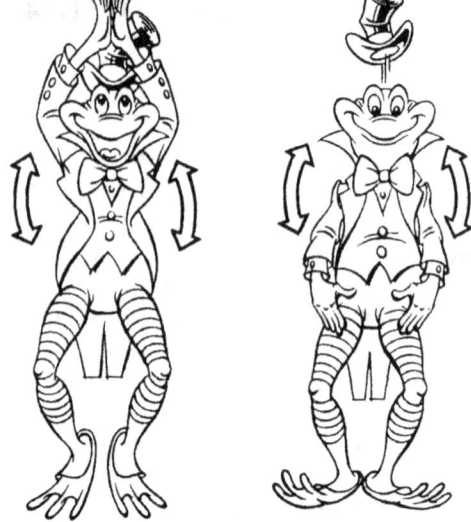

JUMPING JACKS
Stand straight, feet together, arms at sides. When you jump up raise your arms overhead and clap hands together, at the same time spread legs apart sideways. Jump up again, bring arms down to sides and at the same time bring legs together — 8 times.

FROG JUMPS
Squat down to the floor with hands touching the floor. Jump up — 2 times.

Wake Up Little Susie

DR. SWAN: Irwin, I say Irwin!
IRWIN: Yes, Dr. Swan?
SWAN: I think we could do a nice country dance to this one, too —
IRWIN: Well, show us, doctor, show us!
DR. SWAN: Now, let's go with the country jig!
Heel toe, heel toe, skip 1-2-3-4. Heel toe, heel toe, skip 1-2-3-4. Heel toe, heel toe, skip 1-2-3-4. Heel toe, heel toe, skip 1-2-3-4. Yeah, keep it up!
And now skip — skip — skip — keep skipping!
Country jig! Heel toe, heel toe, skip 1-2-3-4. Heel toe, heel toe, skip 1-2-3-4. That's it — that's it! That's it — that's it!
Jump crosses! Jump — cross, jump cross, jump cross, jump cross, jump cross. Good — good!
Country jig! Heel toe, heel toe, skip 1-2-3-4. Heel toe, heel toe, skip 1-2-3-4. Oh you are good — very good!
And now skip — skip — skip — yeah. Skip — skip — skip — whee-ee! Oh wonderful — wonderful!

JUMP CROSSES
Stand straight, jump up, swing your left leg across the right leg. Jump up and do the same with your right leg over your left leg.

COUNTRY JIG

Stand straight, feet together. Point with right heel — then point with right toe. Skip to the right 4 times. Point with left heel — then point with left toe. Skip to the left 4 times. Now repeat with the left foot — then the right foot. Skip to your right 4 times, clap clap. Skip to your left 4 times, clap clap.

Our Lips Are Sealed

IRWIN: Oh, I gotta tell ya — this is one good group! Yes-sir — ree! And you, Dr. Swan, you are the most!
BARNEY: Psst! Hey, Irwin!
IRWIN: Yes, Barney?
BARNEY: Do you mind if I sit this one out?
IRWIN: No, Barney, not at all — if you don't feel well, you SHOULD stop! What's wrong?
BARNEY: Oh, it's not that — I just happened to notice all those books on the shelf over there, and I'd love to sorta browse thru 'em —
IRWIN: Oh — sure — go man — do your thing! Yeah, they don't call you Barney the Book Bear for nothing!
BARNEY: Nobody'll even notice I'm not dancing, and I will be back — promise you won't tell anybody — I don't want people talking about me —
IRWIN: Barney, our lips are sealed!
IRWIN: Hey, where are you, Squeak and Squawk?
SQUAWK: Right over here, Irwin, and ready to go!
IRWIN: Okay! Then go, fellers!
SQUAWK: Right! And we'll start with that old favorite on Mairzy Doats — cross kicks. 1-2-3-4-5-6-7 — 1-2-3-4-5-6-7-8 — SKIP — 1-2-3-4 yeah, that's good —
SQUEAK: Yeah, real good, good — that's good.
SQUEAK: And now, cross kicks 1-2-3-4 — keep it going! — and skip 1-2-3-4-5-6-7-8 — skip — skip — yeah!
SQUAWK: Oh, no, these earth persons are almost as good as folks back home!
SQUAWK: And now step swings! Right-left — right-left — right-left — keep swingin'! And now Donald's favorite: frog jumps! Down-up — down-up — down-up — down-up
SQUEAK: And now back to cross kicks! 1-2-3-4-5-6-7-8 — 1-2-3-4-5-6-7-8 — and skip! Wow! This group is the greatest-eek!
SQUAWK: You said it — awk!

CROSS KICKS
Stand straight, lift up your left leg and kick in front of your right leg. Repeat with your right leg kicking in front of your left.

STEP SWINGS
Stand straight, lift up your left leg and kick in front of your right leg. Repeat with your right leg kicking in front of your left.

FROG JUMP
Squat down to the floor with hands touching the floor. Jump up — 2 times.

Washington Post March

PAN: Oh, Irwin! Are you coming to the school game tomorrow?
IRWIN: You better believe it, Pan!
PAN: Some of the kids didn't believe me when I told them, but they will now! You're going to be the star attraction!
PETER: Yeah — we've got Irwin banners all over the place!
IRWIN: That sounds really exciting, Peter!
PAN: Hey, I got a great idea! Why don't you — ALL come, Squeak and Squawk and Clem and Donald and Barney and Dr. Swan, all you wonderful people!?
IRWIN: Fantastic idea! And let's warm up for the parade right now, to the music of the Washington Post March!
IRWIN: Take it, Pan — it's your parade!
PAN: Okay, everybody — let's MARCH!
HUP-2-3-4 — HUP-2-3-4 —
And now — skip — skip — skip — and now one we've done before — step swings! Right-left, right-left — right-left, right, left — right. Yeah, down-up — down-up — down-up and skip! And now march! — Wow! What a parade! Yeah — and skip — skip — skip — wheee-ee!

MARCH
Stand straight and raise the left knee first up high, then down, then the right knee up high, then down — 42 times.

STEP SWINGS
Stand straight, lift up your left leg and kick in front of your right leg. Repeat with your right leg kicking in front of your left.

STEP SWINGS
Stand straight, lift up your left leg and kick in front of your right leg. Repeat with your right leg kicking in front of your left.

FROG JUMPS
Squat down to the floor with hands touching the floor. Jump up — 2 times.

Alley Cat

IRWIN: Whoo-oo-oo-whee! What a bash!
PAN: Yeah, and our school is going to have the greatest parade in history!
DONALD: First, aerobic dancing, then aerobic cookies —
CLEM: Cookies! Cookies! Yeah, me want cookies!
DONALD: And now aerobic parades! Is there no end to this aerobic thing!
IRWIN: I doubt it, Donald ole buddy — it's the greatest thing to come down the pike since pizza! But I tell ya what you can sit this one out if you like, while we all sorta cool down with our cool little friend, the Alley Cat!
DONALD: Perish, forbid the day should ever come when Donald the Disco Frog doesn't dance at a dance party, any kind of party, any kind of dance! Let's go, everybody — follow me!

DONALD:
Right, side, side — left, side, side —
Right, back, back — left, back, back —
Right, knee, knee — left, knee, knee —
Right knee, left knee, jump-clap and turn: AND REPEAT
Right, side, side — left, side, side —
Right, back, back — left, back, back —
Right, knee, knee — left, knee, knee —
Right knee, left knee, jump-clap and turn
 — Hey, that's cool — just keep repeating the same routine —
Yeah, back in the bayou, everybody does this one — confidentially, I gotta tell ya, the cat species and I look at things kinda differently: when Mr. Alley Cat looks at me, I keep wondering if he's looking at a friend — or his next dinner — ya know what I mean?

STEP RIGHT

Hokey Pokey

IRWIN: Cool, Donald, cool! Gotta tell ya, folks, I don't remember when I've had this much fun! But all good things gotta end some time!
ALL: Aw-ww-ww — no, no, wow-gee —
IRWIN: Well — okay! One more once! For the last dance, let's let it all hang out to one of the first aerobic dances of them all, the Hokey Pokey! Just follow the song — it says it all!
IRWIN: Well, what can I tell ya, you're all just too much! Squeak and Squawk, couldn't have done it without you!

SQUEAK: It was cool, man real cool — eek!
SQUAWK: Yeah, almost as good as back home on Mairzy Doats — awk!
IRWIN: And I want to thank you all for coming: Donald and Barney and Clem and Peter and Pan and Dr. Swan —
DR. SWAN: Wouldn't have missed it for the world!
IRWIN: Well, so long folks, and keep on dancing!

Put your left arm in and you shake it all about.

Put your right foot in and you shake it all about.

Put your left foot in and you shake it all about.

You put your right arm in and you shake it all about.

www.ingramcontent.com/pod-product-compliance
Lightning Source LLC
Chambersburg PA
CBHW051216290426
44109CB00021B/2479